D1506076

Caribou
of the Tundra

By Amy B. Rogers

KidHaven
PUBLISHING

Published in 2018 by
KidHaven Publishing, an Imprint of Greenhaven Publishing, LLC
353 3rd Avenue
Suite 255
New York, NY 10010

Designer: Deanna Paternostro
Editor: Vanessa Oswald

Photo credits: Cover Josef Pittner/Shutterstock.com; p. 5 Dmitry Chulov/Shutterstock.com; pp. 7, 15, 19 Sergey Krasnoshchokov/Shutterstock.com; p. 9 Terence Mendoza/Shutterstock.com; p. 11 Vladimir Wrangel/Shutterstock.com; p. 13 franco lucato/Shutterstock.com; p. 17 seafarer/ Shutterstock.com; p. 21 (top), back cover Mario7/Shutterstock.com; p. 21 (bottom) BlueOrange Studio/Shutterstock.com.

Cataloging-in-Publication Data

Names: Rogers, Amy B.
Title: Caribou of the tundra / Amy B. Rogers.
Description: New York : KidHaven Publishing, 2018. | Series: Animals of the tundra | Includes index.
Identifiers: ISBN 9781534522299 (pbk.) | 9781534522237 (library bound) | ISBN 9781534522183 (6 pack) | ISBN 9781534522190 (ebook)
Subjects: LCSH: Caribou–Juvenile literature.
Classification: LCC QL737.U55 R64 2018 | DDC 599.65'8–dc23
Printed in the United States of America

CPSIA compliance information: Batch #BS17KL: For further information contact Greenhaven Publishing LLC, New York, New York at 1-844-317-7404.

Please visit our website, www.greenhavenpublishing.com. For a free color catalog of all our high-quality books, call toll free 1-844-317-7404 or fax 1-844-317-7405.

Contents

Cool Caribou

Caribou is the name given to wild reindeer in North America. They can be found in the tundra, which is a flat, treeless place with frozen ground. They have **adapted** to living in a cold **climate**.

Caribou are actually a **species** of deer!

Caribou are large animals with **antlers** on their head. The male caribou ram into each other with their antlers. Female caribou are smaller than male caribou.

antlers

Male caribou are as tall as an adult man, but they weigh a lot more!

Caribou's white winter coats, made of fur with **hollow** hairs, keep them warm in the chilly tundra. These coats also **camouflage** caribou, which makes it hard to see them in the snow. In the summer, their coats are brown and store body heat, too.

A caribou's coat helps
it hide in the snow.

9

The hooves of caribou are special because they allow them to walk on ice and rocks. Caribou hooves are hollow on the bottom and act as a big scoop, which they use to dig in the snow for food.

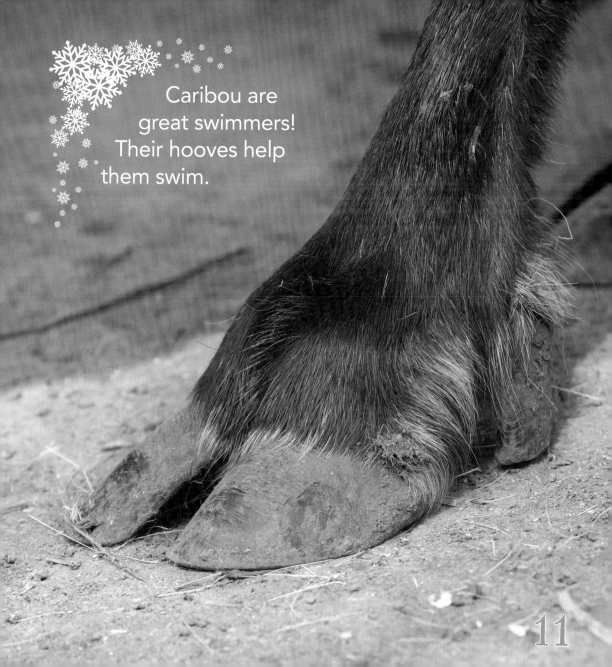

Caribou are great swimmers! Their hooves help them swim.

Finding Food with the Herd

Caribou are herbivores, which means they eat plants. In the summer, they eat grass and plants found in the tundra. In the winter, snow covers most of the tundra, and the caribou go south to find food.

Caribou have
a very good sense
of smell, which helps
them find food.

13

In their search for food, caribou form **herds** of up to 500,000. Together, they travel to forests thousands of miles away. They dig for reindeer moss, which is one of their main sources of food in the winter.

Caribou migrate,
or travel to find food.

15

Caribou Families

In the fall, the male caribou **mate** with the females.

By the spring, young caribou called calves are born.

In the spring, plants are able to grow again in the tundra, and calves grow strong from eating them.

A newborn calf can outrun a person when it's only one day old!

17

Hunters of Caribou

Caribou are **prey** for several animal **predators**, such as bears and wolves. Calves are even more in danger in the first week of their lives. To warn each other of a predator, caribou put their tail in the air, hold their head high, and run.

Caribou also talk to each other through grunts and other sounds.

19

For thousands of years, people have hunted caribou for their meat and fur. Their antlers are used to make tools. They are also great at pulling heavy loads on sleds!

Learning More

How tall are caribou?	up to 5 feet (1.5 m) at the shoulder
How long are caribou?	up to 7 feet (2.1 m)
How much do caribou weigh?	about 700 pounds (320 kg); females are smaller
How long does a caribou live?	about 15 years in the wild
What does a caribou eat?	grass, other plants, and reindeer moss

Caribou are cool animals!

Glossary

adapt: To change to live better in a certain environment.

antler: A bony, branched growth on the head of an animal.

camouflage: To use color or shapes to blend in with the surroundings.

climate: The type of weather in a certain place.

herd: A group of animals that live, feed, or migrate together.

hollow: Having empty space inside.

mate: To come together to make babies.

predator: An animal that feeds on other animals.

prey: An animal hunted by other animals for food.

species: A group of plants or animals that are all the same kind.

For More Information

Websites

National Geographic Kids: Caribou

kids.nationalgeographic.com/animals/caribou/#caribou-standing-grass.jpg
This website provides fun facts about caribou.

National Wildlife Federation

blog.nwf.org/2010/12/reindeer-twelve-fascinating-facts-about-these-amazing-creatures/
The National Wildlife Federation lists 12 things readers should know about caribou.

Books

Johnson, Jinny. *Caribou*. Mankato, MN: Smart Apple Media, 2014.

Owens, Mary Beth. *A Caribou Alphabet*. Thomaston, ME: Tilbury House Publishers, 2015.

Index